Lisa's Inspirations

To: Damota
May this devotional
Bless your life.

Lisa Dixon

4/23/15

Lisa's Inspirations

ISBN-13: 978-0-692-26483-6

All rights reserved. no part of this publication may be reproduced or transmitted in any form or by any means, electronic or mechanical, including photocopy, recording, or any information storage and retrieval system, without the prior permission of the publisher.

Printed in the United States of America

Lisa's Inspirations
A Daily Devotional

Every night before bed, think of one thing you're grateful for that you've never been grateful for before.

GOD HAS A WAY OF TURNING THINGS AROUND FOR YOU.

**"If God is for us, who can be against us?"
Romans 8:31 (NIV)**

DEDICATION

To my weekly text friends and family: You have loved, encouraged and supported me during the writing of what God has put on my heart to share with others. You have been my refocusing source during times of change in my life. With Agape love, I dedicate this book to you.

CONTENTS

Day 1: Questions to Release Your Spiritual Freedom — 1

Day 2: The Woman in the Mirror — 3

Day 3: You're a Holy Temple — 5

Day 4: Worthy or Worthless — 6

Day 5: First Fruit — 7

Day 6: Love Unconditionally — 9

Day 7: Spirit and Truth: My Reflections — 11

Day 8: Pass the Peace — 13

Day 9: Worship in Spirit and in Truth — 14

Day 10: Armor-Bearer — 16

Day 11: Famine in the Church — 18

Day 12: Salt of the Earth: New Assignment — 19

Day 13: Satan's Time — 20

Day 14: What's Shaking Your Ladder? — 21

Day 15: Hungry for God — 22

Day 16: Agape love is from God (Spiritual Love) — 24

Day 17: Living beyond your excuses	25
Day 18: Restoration from Depression	26
Day 19: Prayer for Marriages and Families	29
Day 20: Prayer at the Family Altar	30
Day 21: Setting a time for Prayer	31
Day 22: Prayers and Testimonies	33
Day 23: What to pray for in families: Pray for the Father	34
Day 24: What to Pray for In Families: Pray for the Mother	36
Day 25: What to Pray for in Families: Prayers for the children	39
Day 26: General Prayers	41
Day 27: How to accept the waves of Life	44

DAY 1

Questions to Release Your Spiritual Freedom

Women, these are the questions that can release and deliver you. Seek God and remind yourself to look to God and not others for the answers. Each night, I process who we are as Crown Jewels in my spirit. Each morning, a new revelation is in me that I must share. Take time to answer these questions as the Holy Spirit reveals truth to you.

What is required in a battle to win?
What does it mean to endure to the end?
How high must I go to topple the peak?
How low is the low that threatens my reach?
What number of days are enough to endure?
How saved must I be before I am pure?
How long must I look to see the daylight?
How dark must it get to escape the cold night?
How far must I crawl before I can walk?
How long must I listen before I can talk?
How long do I walk before I can run?
How hard do I work before I am done?
How much pain must I suffer before there's relief?

How much faith do I need to cease unbelief?

How lost must I be before I am found?

How free must I be so as not to be bound?

How many tears have to fall before I stop crying?

How many wounds have to pierce me before I stop dying?

How lonely must I get before comfort is felt?

How many hills must I look to before I see help?

> **Scripture: 2 Corinthians 3:17**
> Now the Lord is the Spirit, and where the Spirit of the Lord is, there is freedom.

DAY 2

The Woman in the Mirror

Do you know who you are? Be the person God wants you to be. Take a true look at yourself. Study your reflection. What do you see? Becoming the person you want to be is a process. See the woman in the mirror you want to be, and be her.

The book of Esther reminds us of our call and our purpose. Learn to love yourself (Esther 2:12). Have confidence in yourself and who you are. Have high self esteem, and don't downplay your skills and talents. You need to correct people when they are not speaking of the true you. What information are you holding back? Get over people and what they think about you.

Instead of considering what others think of you, devote your time to examining yourself. Are you playing a role? When you look in the mirror, do you see yourself? (Ephesians 4:12) Find your call, develop your gifts and walk in what God wants you to be. God is your everything. Learn what God has called you to do. Be satisfied with your reflection in the mirror.

When God places a call on your life, it is up to you to answer the call. Be ready to do what God has called you to do.

God positions you to serve Him at work, in the community and abroad. What major impact do you have in the kingdom of God? Don't lose sight of yourself by seeing through the eyes of others. Acting is hard! Be yourself, and be real. Learn to truly love God with all your heart, mind and soul. Our deepest fear is that we are powerful beyond our eyes. You must not be small in God. By letting your light shine, you can overcome all of your insecurities.

> **Scripture: Ester 2:12**
> Before a young woman's turn came to go in to King Xerxes, she had to complete twelve months of beauty treatments prescribed for the women, six months with oil of myrrh and six with perfumes and cosmetics.

DAY 3

You're a Holy Temple

Understand you are a Holy Temple (1 Corinthians 3:16). Temples are not built overnight. It takes time to become a good temple. Understand your process with God. A temple is a building and a place where wars are won. When a battle is won, victory is yours.

> **Scripture: 1 Corinthians 3:16**
> Don't you know that you yourselves are God's temple and that God's Spirit dwells in your midst?

DAY 4

Worthy or Worthless

Worthless means of no use, good for nothing, empty and without purpose. Worthy means fit (Matthew 8:8), qualified, adequate and competent (2 Corinthians 2:16). Let God's mind be in you. Make decisions to move forward in your life. Don't see yourself for where you are now but where God would have you to be in royalty. Understand that God has more in store for you. A zero that stands alone has no value, but a zero placed in the right spot or situation adds great value to its location. Right decisions lead to right action and right character.

> **Scripture: 2 Corinthians 2:16**
> To the one we are an aroma that brings death; to the other, an aroma that brings life. And who is equal to such a task?

DAY 5
First Fruit

Something that is first comes before all else. Fruit is the result of effort. It is produce that grows out of a planted seed. It is the direct result of something that was done before. First fruit describes the first fruit of the first harvest.

Sometimes we need to look at the historical evidence and other educational material available to help us understand certain things from historical and cultural perspectives. History gives us the opportunity to gain the full impact of the meaning of scripture. For example, the concept of first fruit would leave someone mystified today unless they had an agricultural background or understanding.

God commanded His people to present the first fruit to the Leviticus priesthood, and this first fruit served as their food (Deuteronomy 26:2). In Israel, first fruit marked the end of the barley growing season and the beginning of the wheat season.

The following scriptures reference first fruit.

And the feast of harvest, the first fruits of thy labors, which thou hast sown in the field: and the feast of ingathering, which is in the end of the year, when thou hast gathered in thy labors out of the field (Exodus 23:16 NKJV).

The first of the first fruits of thy land thou shalt bring into the house of the LORD thy God. Thou shalt not seethe a kid in his mother's milk (Exodus 23:19 KJV).

> **Scripture: Galatians 5:22-23**
> But the fruit of the Spirit is love, joy, peace, forbearance, kindness, goodness, faithfulness, gentleness and self-control. Against such things there is no law.

DAY 6

Love Unconditionally

God has really been speaking to me about loving unconditionally. I am to choose to love others no matter what, even through the hurts. As I pray for you and you pray for me, let us ask our God to empower us to love our brothers and sisters no matter the situation.

I may be able to speak the languages of human beings and even of angels, but if I have no love, my speech is no more than a noisy gong or a clanging bell.

I may have the gift of inspired preaching; I may have all knowledge and understand all secrets; I may have all the faith needed to move mountains-but if I have no love, I am nothing. I may give away everything I have, and even give up my body to be burned-but if I have no love, this does me no good. Love is patient and kind; it is not jealous or conceited or proud;

Love is not ill-mannered or selfish or irritable; love does not keep a record of wrongs; Love is not happy with evil, but is happy with the truth. Love never gives up; and its faith, hope, and patience never fail. Love is eternal (1 Corinthians 13: 1-8 GNT).

But I tell everyone who is listening: Love your enemies. Be kind to those who hate you. Bless those who curse you. Pray for those who insult you. If someone strikes you on the cheek, offer the other cheek as well. If someone takes your coat, don't stop him from taking your shirt. Give to everyone who asks you for something. If someone takes what is yours, don't insist on getting it back. Do for other people everything you'd like them to do for you (Luke 6:27-31).

Scripture: 1 Corinthians 13:4-7

Love is patient, love is kind. It does not envy, it does not boast, it is not proud. It does not dishonor others, it is not self-seeking, it is not easily angered, it keeps no record of wrongs. Love does not delight in evil but rejoices with the truth. It always protects, always trusts, always hopes, always perseveres.

DAY 7

Spirit and Truth: My Reflections

It takes total commitment to faith and the Word of God to order the steps to God servitude. We must learn to shake away the doubts and fears, step out there and use the gifts that God has given us to uplift His kingdom. The problem some of us have is that we want to lead rather than serve. We are most humble when we dare to take care of our fellow brothers and sisters. That's what being in service for God is all about.

Twelve disciples sought God through faith. The kingdom was made new because they understood their call. God wants us to become a ministry in ourselves by spending time in His word and doing His will.

You cannot hear God clearly when you are tired and surrounded by noise. God will take you, voluntarily or involuntarily, to a quiet place so He can speak to you. We must understand that we are royal people in charge and responsible for God's purpose.

In the next three days God will show Himself in the fullest of your life. All of your questions will be answered. Assess what you have! Use those things in the kingdom of

God for His glory. Let your light shine for God, and always give Him thanks.

My job is to win souls for Christ Jesus. The joy of working with God's people in their spiritual walk is like no other. Disciples cannot eat first. They must feed others before feeding themselves. When you minister, be yourself and feed God's people with His word for their lives. We must share God's word with others. It's our responsibility.

Scripture: **John 4:24**
God is spirit, and his worshipers must worship in the Spirit and in truth."

DAY 8

Pass the Peace

Problems at one level need to be resolved on a higher level. God will reveal an earthly problem that can only be solved with a kingdom solution. Change the word over your life by speaking life to death situations. Spiritual wisdom is a must! To have wisdom of the natural and spiritual world is to have great insight. Our time has come to have a clear understanding of what God wants us to do. Change the way you think. Refuse to stay in a problematic situation *(Mark 4:30, Matthew 11:7, Daniel 1:3, Daniel 4:3, Luke 16: 1-31, Amos 3:7)*.

> ### Scripture: **Psalm 29:11**
> The Lord gives strength to his people;
> > the Lord blesses his people with peace.

DAY 9

Worship in Spirit and in Truth

What is worship? Worship is a one-on-one relationship with God. It is seeking God's attention everyday of your life. The foundation of worship is to be intimate with God daily. True worshipers have a personal relationship with God. They totally rely on God and not the flesh, and they confess confidence in God.

Worship teams should be considered as ***worship leaders***. Worship leaders are sensitive to the moving of the Spirit; therefore, their leading of worship flows with the Spirit. It is real and not staged. We must worship with the anticipation of intimacy. Through worship, we are transformed. Move past seeking God's hand and seek His face. God knows you through your personal relationship with Him.

Seek God's understanding when you worship in music and dance. He will give you understanding for your life. Move forward in your authority in worship. Make your ministry real. Move forward in true understanding of what God is saying to you for the salvation of others.

If you are worshiping in truth, your worship will be seen in the eyes of God and others. A lie will be exposed. If you are not true in the Spirit, it will be exposed. Seek God to help you worship in spirit and in truth. Remember, people are hungry for God in their lives.

> **Scripture: John 4:23-24**
> Yet a time is coming and has now come when the true worshipers will worship the Father in the Spirit and in truth, for they are the kind of worshipers the Father seeks. God is spirit, and his worshipers must worship in the Spirit and in truth.

DAY 10
Armor-Bearer

You must be complete in order to be used by someone else for kingdom building. You must be mature to understand that someone else's vision and purpose comes first. You must be prepared for the call to serve as a true armor-bearer. Your heart must be connected with the spirit of the one for whom you are serving. This walk is about the spiritual joining, and it moves by the Spirit of God. You walk in the same mind and heart for fulfilling God's purpose.

Armor-bearer is a call to a person and not a place. There must be a willingness to lay down your life, vision and dreams for the one you are serving as an armor-bearer. You must be connected in the spirit to the people God assigns you to serve. You must stay close to see what they see. Follow them, be with them and stand with them. Add strength.

> **Scripture: 1 Samuel 31:4**
>
> Saul said to his armor-bearer, "Draw your sword and run me through, or these uncircumcised fellows will come and run me through and abuse me."
>
> But his armor-bearer was terrified and would not do it; so Saul took his own sword and fell on it.

Sometimes the people of God you serve may not greet you, but it is not personal. They have many things on their minds, so don't be hurt or touched by this action (Romans 14:17). Make sure your inner conversation matches your outer conversation (John 6:60-66). True discipleship examines us daily. Take the risk of being rejected. Offer encouragement daily to support the people of God. Stay faithful to them (Judges 9:53-54, 1 Samuel 14:6-7).

DAY 11

Famine in the Church

The church needs to move on and celebrate a new level of God. If we stay in our same condition (in flesh), the church will not grow. Churches that aren't growing emit a bad odor, and new members cannot tolerate the smell of stagnation and traditionalism. They cannot stand the show, and they desire a worship experience that is authentic in spirit and truth. Connect yourself to God and see what word He has for you. Obeying God is a must. If you don't, God will break you through the spirit.

The place of anointing (healing pool) moves in the authority that God gave you for His will. Support what God is doing for His people. Align yourself with what God is doing in the Kingdom (2 Kings 6:25, Hebrews 12:28-29).

> **Scripture: Amos 8:11**
>
> "The days are coming," declares the Sovereign Lord,
>
> "when I will send a famine through the land—
>
> not a famine of food or a thirst for water,
>
> but a famine of hearing the words of the Lord.

DAY 12

Salt of the Earth: New Assignment

Maximize changes in your life, but know that the church will not understand you. Change the people around you so God can move in and through your life. Transform to your new place even when you're under attack. This is when God is moving in your life. God is setting you up. God is preparing you for greatness.

Flow in your anointing when God is feeding you. We will hear things that are not of this world. God feeds our spirits daily. God works on our brokenness and directs our paths for His will. Whatever we feed on will grow in our lives. Whatever we resist will die in our lives. God is preparing us to grow by feeding us. Allow God to feed you so your will for God can come forth. Prayer is the answer.

> **Scripture: Matthew 5:13**
> "You are the salt of the earth. But if the salt loses its saltiness, how can it be made salty again? It is no longer good for anything, except to be thrown out and trampled underfoot.

DAY 13

Satan's Time

Attack is not a bad thing. Attack means it's time to shift. God will use an attack in His favor for His will. Your enemies will bless you. You will grow more with the attacks of Satan than you will without them. It is good to have people like John and Judas in your life. Change is coming. You have outgrown where you are in the ministry. God is getting ready to move you to the next level. There is no room for God if you are stuck in the pride of life. God's grace should bring you to your knees. Fall down on your knees. Let God's will be done in your life.

> **Scripture: Job 1:8**
> \Then the LORD said to Satan, "Have you considered my servant Job? There is no one on earth like him; he is blameless and upright, a man who fears God and shuns evil."

DAY 14

What's Shaking Your Ladder?

Find your way back from shame. Take off your shame and walk in your glory. You cannot fix the problem until you face it (Galatians 6:1). God and His mercy have covered us all the days of our lives. Don't compare your spiritual walk with others. God has a plan for you. Consider the experiences of David and Peter. Your shame is no worse than theirs. If God forgave them, He can forgive you and He has. Walk in your forgiveness and authority for the purpose of God.

Everything works out for your good. I want God's true anointing to consume me, so I can do what God would have me to do in His kingdom. Don't allow the world to tell you what you can and cannot have. God has the answers for your life (Psalm 73:17, Luke 22:67).

> **Scripture: Psalm 73:17**
>
> till I entered the sanctuary of God;
>
> > then I understood their final destiny.

DAY 15

Hungry for God

Your womb needs to be strong to handle what God is bringing to your life. You must have endurance and be able to stand firm. Never give up! (Matthew 7:24-25, Genesis 28: 1-22). Be hungry for God. Others are not hungry for God, and that is why their lives are filled with mess. Build yourself up, and purge yourself of anything that's not of God (Matthew 15:21-28, 2 Kings 19: 1-37).

> ### Scripture: **Matthew 15:21-28**
> Leaving that place, Jesus withdrew to the region of Tyre and Sidon. A Canaanite woman from that vicinity came to him, crying out, "Lord, Son of David, have mercy on me! My daughter is demon-possessed and suffering terribly."
>
> Jesus did not answer a word. So his disciples came to him and urged him, "Send her away, for she keeps crying out after us."

24 He answered, "I was sent only to the lost sheep of Israel."
25 The woman came and knelt before him. "Lord, help me!" she said.

[26] He replied, "It is not right to take the children's bread and toss it to the dogs."

[27] "Yes it is, Lord," she said. "Even the dogs eat the crumbs that fall from their master's table."

[28] Then Jesus said to her, "Woman, you have great faith! Your request is granted." And her daughter was healed at that moment.

DAY 16

Agape love is from God (Spiritual Love)

God is love. No love, no power; no word, no faith; no love, no anointing. Human emotional love is conditional love. No results, no Holy Ghost. Develop in the love of God. Stand strong and die to yourself, so that God can live in you. You must love the Lord with all your heart and walk in the love of God. To love is a true work of God.

The **Word** is the seed of God. It is word seed and not money seed. Word seed controls all increase in the kingdom of God. The word of God will determine how you think (Genesis 12: 1-20). Be careful and watch your associates at all times. Pay attention to the people around you. The way you think is reflected in how you live. Do not allow your emotions to have control over you. Regardless of what people are saying, continue to smile and walk in your authority with God. God wants some Christians who think before they act!

> **Scripture: John 13:34-35**
> "A new command I give you: Love one another. As I have loved you, so you must love one another. By this everyone will know that you are my disciples, if you love one another.

DAY 17

Living beyond your excuses

Change, expand and grow **now!** To live out your dreams, you must get past the excuses. The plans God has for you are far greater than the plans we have for ourselves. We must get over the excuses. Excuses will rob you of your faith. The life that God has put in you is bigger than the one we live in now. Don't be afraid of failure, and don't hang around with people who have given up on their dreams (Ephesians 2:10). You are the workmanship of God. There is something good about you. You are anointed to do something in this world for the glory of God. How far do you want to go? How big is your vision? God will only take you as far as you are prepared to go. You must get past your excuses. Dare to be different! (St Luke 14:16).

> ### Scripture: **1 Corinthians 15:31**
> I face death every day—yes, just as surely as I boast about you in Christ Jesus our Lord.

DAY 18

Restoration from Depression

Depression is anger turned inward. When expectation and reality come together, it is a reality check. The spirit of heaviness comes in when our hearts are hurt. Heaviness steals your joy and puts you in the wrong state of being. A negative spirit overtakes you. Don't settle for less in this life. Take authority. You have authority to move in all that God has for you. Our job is to bring people out of heaviness and into the light of Jesus Christ for the glory of God. God will fulfill His promise in your life for His glory (Isaiah 61:1-3).

> **Scripture: 1 Kings 19:5-18**
>
> Then he lay down under the bush and fell asleep.
>
> All at once an angel touched him and said, "Get up and eat." He looked around, and there by his head was some bread baked over hot coals, and a jar of water. He ate and drank and then lay down again.
>
> The angel of the Lord came back a second time and touched him and said, "Get up and eat, for the journey is too much for you."

So he got up and ate and drank. Strengthened by that food, he traveled forty days and forty nights until he reached Horeb, the mountain of God. There he went into a cave and spent the night.

The Lord Appears to Elijah

And the word of the Lord came to him: "What are you doing here, Elijah?"

He replied, "I have been very zealous for the Lord God Almighty. The Israelites have rejected your covenant, torn down your altars, and put your prophets to death with the sword. I am the only one left, and now they are trying to kill me too."

The Lord said, "Go out and stand on the mountain in the presence of the Lord, for the Lord is about to pass by."

Then a great and powerful wind tore the mountains apart and shattered the rocks before the Lord, but the Lord was not in the wind. After the wind there was an earthquake, but the Lord was not in the earthquake. After the earthquake came a fire, but the Lord was not in the fire. And after the fire came a gentle whisper. When Elijah heard it, he pulled his cloak over his face and went out and stood at the mouth of the cave.

Then a voice said to him, "What are you doing here, Elijah?"

Lisa's Inspirations: A Daily Devotional

He replied, "I have been very zealous for the Lord God Almighty. The Israelites have rejected your covenant, torn down your altars, and put your prophets to death with the sword. I am the only one left, and now they are trying to kill me too."

The Lord said to him, "Go back the way you came, and go to the Desert of Damascus. When you get there, anoint Hazael king over Aram. Also, anoint Jehu son of Nimshi king over Israel, and anoint Elisha son of Shaphat from Abel Meholah to succeed you as prophet. Jehu will put to death any who escape the sword of Hazael, and Elisha will put to death any who escape the sword of Jehu. Yet I reserve seven thousand in Israel—all whose knees have not bowed down to Baal and whose mouths have not kissed him."

DAY 19

Prayer for Marriages and Families

There is an immense attack on family life. There has probably never been a time in history when marriages and families have been under such strain. Purposeful, systematic, intelligent and persevering prayer is necessary in this area.

> **Scripture: 1 Corinthians 7:39**
> A woman is bound to her husband as long as he lives. But if her husband dies, she is free to marry anyone she wishes, but he must belong to the Lord.

DAY 20

Prayer at the Family Altar

It is important that each family prays together. Husbands and wives should pray together regularly. There should be a scheduled time each day when the whole family prays together and studies the Word of God. Rosalind Rinker's "Prayer: *Conversing with God*" is an excellent family resource and worth reading as you establish a standard of prayer for your family.

Create an atmosphere for Bible study and prayer in the home. Prayer should be the natural answer for any matter in the home. In a crisis, thank the Lord for an answer to prayer, or admonish Him for who He is and what He has done.

> **Scripture: Hebrews 13:10**
> We have an altar from which those who minister at the tabernacle have no right to eat.

DAY 21
Setting a time for Prayer

There must be a specific time and place for family prayer. The specified time should be established to accommodate everybody, and everybody should know this is the time the family collectively fellowships with God. Encourage everyone to write their prayer requests in a family prayer journal, and be sure to enter the answers regularly. This practice builds faith and teaches our families to thank God for His answers.

It is also meaningful to have a system for specific prayers concerning the family. Create a prayer schedule. For instance, pray for the authorities on Monday and devote Tuesday to prayer for your minister/pastor and a missionary adopted by the family. On Wednesday pray for unsaved people. Each family can create a system and prayer schedule.

Each member of the family must participate in prayer. Don't force anybody to pray; each member must do it out of his or her free will. Practice continued prayer. Each person can pray for one item at a time, and the others can join in silent prayer. Also, each member of the family can choose an issue for which to pray on that occasion.

> ### Scripture: **Matthew 6:6**
> But when you pray, go into your room, close the door and pray to your Father, who is unseen. Then your Father, who sees what is done in secret, will reward you.

DAY 22

Prayers and Testimonies

Share answers that you have received on prayer requests throughout the day with family members. This practice builds recognition of God's power and increases the faith of the family while giving family members more confidence to ask God for specific things as well. When we pray for specific things, we expect specific answers. The family prayer is not a substitute for your personal quiet time. The following elements are important for family prayer.

- ♦ Praise and Worship
- ♦ Thanksgiving
- ♦ Personal requests by different members of the family
- ♦ Praying scripture
- ♦ Intercession for the outside world, unsaved people and the poor

> **Scripture: Matthew 26:37**
> He took Peter and the two sons of Zebedee along with him, and he began to be sorrowful and troubled.

DAY 23

What to pray for in families: *Pray for the Father*

- Pray that he will love his wife as Christ loved the church.

"Husbands, love your wives just as Christ loved the church and gave Himself up for her ... husbands ought to love their wives as their own bodies... he feeds and cares for it, just as Christ does the church" (Ephesians 5:25-32 NLT).

"Husbands, love your wives and do not be harsh with them" (Colossians 3:19 NIV).

"Husbands in the same way be considerate as you live with your wives and treat them with respect as the weaker partner and as heirs with you of the gracious gift of life so that nothing will hinder your prayers" (1 Peter 3:7 NIV).

- Pray that the father will be the priest in the home by giving guidance and praying for his family.
- Pray that the father will exercise his authority given to him by God and not leave it to his wife.
- Pray that the husband will be reasonable toward his wife.

- Pray that he will be patient with his wife and have self control with his family.
- Pray that the husband will be aware of his wife's needs for love, safety and security as well as her other needs. Pray that he will pay attention to them.
- Pray that he will exercise spiritual and social leadership and that he will provide for his family.

> **Scripture: Deuteronomy 1:29-31**
>
> Then I said to you, "Do not be terrified; do not be afraid of them. The Lord your God, who is going before you, will fight for you, as he did for you in Egypt, before your very eyes, and in the wilderness. There you saw how the Lord your God carried you, as a father carries his son, all the way you went until you reached this place."

DAY 24

What to Pray for In Families: Pray for the Mother

- Pray that she will submit to her husband in everything as the church is submissive to Christ (Ephesians 5:22-24).

"Wives in the same way submit yourselves to your own husbands so that if any of them do not believe the Word they may be won over without words by the behavior of their wives when they see the purity and reverence of your lives. Your beauty should not come from outward adornment such as braided hair and the wearing of gold jewelry and fine clothes" (1 Peter 3:1-3 NIV).

"...the wife must respect her husband" (Ephesians 5:33 NIV).

- Pray for a quiet and gentle spirit and that she will know when to keep quiet. Pray for the wife's patience with her husband.
- Pray that she will respect her husband and that she will not try to dominate or prescribe to him.
- Pray that she will not complain about her husband but will respect him and try to meet his needs.

- Pray that the wife will accept her husband's leadership.
- Pray that the wife will realize that her husband is a fellow sinner and that she will have patience with his faults. Pray that she will allow him the freedom to be himself.
- Specifically pray against a domineering attitude in the wife, especially in cases where she is spiritually stronger than her husband. This can cause endless damage to the children. Also, pray against any form of manipulation from the wife. Manipulation is always negative.

THE VALUE OF MOTHERS

Mothers are so many things. They are mentors, motivational speakers and mood regulators. Mothers are masterful, mighty and memorable, but most of all mothers are our miracle.

Mothers were created to be observers and occupational therapists. They are open-minded and original.

Mothers are teachers, trainers, trustworthy tactical organizers and triumphant in the most difficult of situations.

Moms are honest, hospitable and honorable. They are humanitarians and everyday heroes.

Mommas are economists, enthusiasts, encouragers and entertainers. They exceed expectations and are extraordinary to those they touch.

Mothers are resilient, respected, regarded and resourceful. They should be rewarded as they have been remarkable.

You see, a mother is not just limited to caring for or giving birth to a child. She is so much more. She is God's gift to us. She gives us life and gives us the tools to make it through life. She is the memory that carries us through life. Simply put, she is a gift of love to those she touches.

If your mom is alive, give her your love and respect today and every day. If she has passed on, give that love to someone who has been these things in your life. Whether you have children by birth or adoption or you have natural or spiritual children, you are reverenced and honored. I am sending love and a prayer of richness and abundance to you.

> **Scripture: Proverbs 31:30-31**
>
> Charm is deceptive, and beauty is fleeting;
>
> > but a woman who fears the Lord is to be praised.
>
> Honor her for all that her hands have done,
>
> > and let her works bring her praise at the city gate.

DAY 25

What to Pray for in Families: Prayers for the children

- Pray for obedience and submissiveness to the parents.
- Pray for their salvation and for the spiritual growth of those already saved.
- Pray for their physical growth, health and good eating habits.
- Pray for their education and sports activities.
- Pray for their intellectual development and for their growth in wisdom and knowledge.
- Pray for the figures of authority with which they have daily contact, including teachers, sports coaches, parents, grandparents, etc.
- Pray for their social development and for a pure walk in life so that they may discern between right and wrong. Pray that they will be able to resist temptation and that they will choose the right friends.
- Resist the evil one who will try to destroy their lives.

- While they're young, begin to pray for the right choice of careers and marriage partners.
- Pray that they will love God and His Word, and also pray for their joy in life.

> **Scripture: Psalm 127:3**
>
> Children are a heritage from the Lord,
>
> offspring a reward from him.

DAY 26:

General Prayers

- Pray against the spirit of divorce, lust and impurity.
- Especially pray against the following sins and that the Holy Spirit will convict people of these and that they will turn from them: homosexuality, cohabitation, adultery, child molestation, suicide, alcohol and drug abuse.
- Pray against the involvement of a third party in the marriage.
- Pray for an open relationship and good communication in the marriage.
- Pray for deep conviction of sin and that the husband and wife will walk in faith together.
- Pray for understanding of each other's needs and the ability and willingness to meet those needs.
- Pray against every form of selfishness, self-indulgence and willfulness in the marriage.
- Pray that there will be no misunderstandings.

The single, biggest problem in marriages is misunderstanding.

- When there are specific problems in the marriage, such as jealousy, alcohol abuse and extra-marital relationships, one must pray specifically for these matters.
- Pray for the parents in their raising and handling of their children.
- Pray for forgiveness between husbands and wives.
- Pray for widowers, widows and couples who are unable to have children.
- Pray for children without parents and children in orphanages.
- Pray for the single and lonely people who long for the security of a family.
- Pray for children who have run away from home and for children whose friends have a bad influence on them.

Scripture: **Psalms 5:1-3**

Listen to my words, Lord,

    consider my lament.

Hear my cry for help,

    my King and my God,

    for to you I pray.

In the morning, Lord, you hear my voice;

    in the morning I lay my requests before you

    and wait expectantly.

DAY 27:

How to accept the waves of Life

The secret to life is accepting what GOD has for us with a smile. Whatever it is He can see us through it.

God, we reflect on your word in 1 Corinthian 13. It reminds us how God so loved the world totally and unconditionally, so should we continue to love our neighbors, friends, families and co-workers unconditionally. When we show them unconditional love, we show the love of Christ Jesus. He prefects all that concerns us. Believe without sight is just that Belief.

> **Scripture: 1 Thessalonians 5:18**
> Give thanks in all circumstances; for this is God's will for you in Christ Jesus.

Made in the USA
Middletown, DE
17 March 2015